AfterLife

AfterLife

Kathryn Lomer

PUNCHER & WATTMANN

First published in 2023
Published by Puncher and Wattmann
PO Box 279
Waratah NSW 2298

https://www.puncherandwattmann.com
web@puncherandwattmann.com

ISBN   9781922571700

Cover design by Miranda Douglas
Typesetting by Morgan Arnett
Printed by Lightning Source International

NATIONAL LIBRARY OF AUSTRALIA   A catalogue record for this work is available from the National Library of Australia

Stay with things. Engage with the world in meaningful, non-utilitarian ways.

Heidegger

The texture of consciousness is the language of literature not the data of science.

Neurologist, Robert Burton

The world was lovely, really, but it was tricky, and peevish with the small things, like a god who didn't get out much.

Lorrie Moore

The truth of this is simple and profound; how else may we be said to live, except by feeling?

Antonio Damasio – The strange order of things

There are only two ways to live your life. One is as though nothing is a miracle. The other is as though everything is a miracle.

Albert Einstein

Contents

1. Shifting sands

2. Afterlife

3. Vapour trails

4. Trick of light

5. Footpaths of desire

Shifting sands

A hummingbird in Italy

*There are occasional reports of hummingbirds in Europe, but these would
have to be cage birds that have escaped captivity.*

Sailing sedate, dolphins in our wake,
        we come to Ancona singing *Gaudete*.
The clatter of silver on wood;
        my first fresh-picked pomegranate.

Europe's unquiet cuts into dreams:
        Dresden's dead, Jewish dread. I wake first.
Beyond our window, a hummingbird,
        brain the size of a grain of rice,

wings a blur of back and forth.
        Form follows function, this creature dedicated to flight.
How does my body tell me what *I* am for?
        The pillow stuffed with Spanish Lace,

its fragrance mingling with dopamine.
        The things we don't notice:
motion eight milliseconds behind colour.
        You glimpse my crimson coat, leaving,

then sleep on, sleep of the innocent.
        In the north of our country, hot air rises;
monsoons race in to fill the void.
        As with us. If you give up one thing,

you must replace it with another.
        I smell trouble the way kangaroos smell water,
and set out to find it. The bird hovers
        at the glass of a French door left ajar.

I find a bar and, although it's morning,
         people are drinking. I join them.
A glass of wine before breakfast:
         I'm breaking all the rules,

enjoying that thin edge of the wedge.
         I was tired of the brand of hit-and-run loving
available down my street,
         the fine line between rake and rent-boy

and was counselled that marriage had the gentle strength
         of mushrooms pushing up a sack of shit.
Birds follow ultraviolet paths of urine,
         understand chemical conversations in the streets.

They hear infra-sounds of thunderstorms.
         Intuition: our senses working overtime
but we never trust it. 'It's the lore of the jungle', you say,
         spelling it out in case I don't get it.

I try to tidy up my mind:
         hippocampus for mental maps, amygdala for fear,
cingulate gyrus for attention, thalamus...
         I was never good at housekeeping.

Oh, where is my hummingbird harbinger?
         'Friends, freedom and reflection', you said. 'It's Epicurus.'
So many 'f's, I thought. What's that about?
         Words I love: *eros*, *thanatos*;

a thing I love: a carob pod from Patmos.
         The man who gave it said his father died

spreadeagled on an olive tree, taken in the act
> of picking, and everyone thought he was meditating

on the olive caught between finger and thumb.
> Elephants never stop growing (like whales);
free to be as big as they can be.
> My love for the world is like that.

You say I'm a coelacanth, *the fish that time forgot,*
> remembering details like some non-literate.
As though gathering evidence.
> What if, like the bees, we danced our meanings?

Like Zorba? Whirling dervishes?
> My memory is as long as the ever-growing elephant's,
touch remembered in the body.
> I think of Cleopatra and Julius Caesar:

was it love, necessity, compromise?
> Or Sheba and Solomon, together for three years,
composing riddles to test compatibility.
> The hummingbird appears outside the bar window

and hovers, seeing a strange creature
> with ultra-violet hair and fingernails
clutching a swirl of light.
> Ghosts from other times also grow upon me:

I am their private caryatid, a pillar of flesh.
> Maybe the bird sees them, too.
Or does he mistake his reflection for a mate?
> This also happens.

Today I'm feeling the weight of Noah's coupledom;
why *does* everything have to come in twos?
How to be as unerring in love as the Wandering Albatross
with its gentle gift of grass and hooked caress?

But that's as absurd as the hopes invested in a dress.
Remember the one I wore when we married?
It was cream and green with roses.
Words line themselves up like children in a schoolyard.

I say to those children, *young hearts run free.*
When I return and wake you with a kiss, I will try
not to tell you that three hundred kinds of bacteria shared it.
Too much detail! And no god in sight.

History weighs into the present: I no longer say I love you,
part of my diction forever parenthesised.
Perhaps if I find a song with heartbeat minims and quaver kisses,
I'll remember how to sing it.

There'll be a sift and sort of telling pasts,
plain arrangements for the future.
You are already building a black pearl
around my misdeeds. This is one.

Drawing life

We are out of our comfort zone, well out;
if we were swimming, we'd be over our heads,
in the deep end; it's a baptism of fire.
Oh let's mix our metaphors, since everything's
up for grabs; I feel my brain cells realigning.
Really, we're drawing portraits.
But we are very afraid.
We have been drawing this woman's body
for days, noting the ways her hip creates a line
towards her waist, or her scapula foreshortens
from the side. Her pubic bone juts
at an angle if you are in the corner,
under the street windows. A twist here
and a whole different set of shadows arrives
as if the sun itself has shifted.
She has us entranced:
the way her lashes lie against her cheek,
the way, every few minutes, she wets her lips
with her tongue.
She has posed like a statue, but her head is teeming.
One day, there are tears in her eyes.
What if we could draw her thoughts?
It's all an impossible task,
like trying to parse butterflies.
All we can do is begin.
and see how things turn out.

The GOMA man

At GOMA, I see a man who looks just like you
and I follow him all morning.
He walks like you, leaning a little forward into life,
up on the balls of his feet, as if on a rocky boat.
I follow him to Bharti Kher's *The skin speaks a language of its own*
and we stand on opposite sides of the sleeping elephant.
I wonder if this man knows that about skin.
I don't approach him; I only want to savour his likeness.
He is nearby when I sit to eat Thai food as part of *Lunchbox*,
a tableau which mimics our Saturday lunches,
you with your dark ale and us sitting in courtyard sun.
Back at home, I take a friend and stay at your house
one weekend when you're away with your new lover.
I still have a key, remember; for years this was a home to me, too.
I want to finish the book I was reading about the history of numbers.
I want to see if the chocolate-coloured peacock feather is still beside your bed.
I want to see if you have replanted basil in the blue pot I gave you,
if the photograph of your wife is where it always was
and if you've completed the song to the Chinese girl you wish you'd slept with.
I want to light a fire in your tall hearth and sleep in front of it.
I want to stop your cats from straying at night and killing skinks.
I want to sleep in your bed and breathe in your smell.
But there is no smell, and there is no feather.
The pot is desolate, the photograph gone.
The cats do what they like.
And the sun in the courtyard has turned a sour yellow.
If only someone told me it's bad luck to keep peacock feathers in a house;
that giving knives as a gift spells the end of a love affair.
If only I'd asked all the right questions and you'd been able to answer any of them.
If only your thoughts and my feelings had coincided.

If only you'd loved me.
I've been reading a book about wisdom
and I understand it is not wise to break into your former lover's house
or to think of him every single day when you wake
or to continue in your heartbreak for as long as grief
or to try to understand the inscrutable emotions of another.
I know the wise thing is to be kind to yourself and move on.
Wisdom can take a long time.
At the end of the weekend, we discover you in your study.
You have been there all along, listening as we played your piano,
cooked in your kitchen, lit your fire and drank your wine.
You preferred to stay there the whole time, sleep there,
than come out and look at what you've done.
I traipse after the GOMA man all the way to the escalator.
At the top, an artwork on the wall above him, in hot pink neon:
I never stopped loving you.
I let him go.

N.B. GOMA: Gallery of Modern Art, Brisbane; *I never stopped loving you* is by
Tracey Emin.

The glass frog

The glass frog's crimson heart beats
forty times a minute.
And I can see it.
Light shines right through her
and there is the heart beating.
She is the size of a human fingernail,
lost in forest understorey.
A single footfall could crush a hundred
of her kind.
I wish I'd known sooner about the glass frog,
that something so transparent and crushable
lives extravagantly in the midst of lush life.
Fear never enters into it.

Climbing Bishop and Clerk

Listen for the sound of a thousand butterfly wings readying themselves for flight.
Tread quietly on the forest path and leave everything else behind.
Concentration is required, and a quietness of mind. These wings whisper

on the warm breeze of an Indian summer, open in unexpected sunshine.
They lift as I pass, a delicate cloud of white-spotted browns, and jink across my path,
dusting pheromones about my head. This short span of time is everything:

fulfilment of that awkward metamorphosis from cocoon into wild, brief life.
Their wings whisper what butterflies know and I am listening. I am breaking
from my cocoon and climbing mountains, giddy with space and light and movement,

giddy with wonder at everything I see: butterflies; wedge-tailed eagles
hunting overhead; wombats intent on grass; forester kangaroos leaping through scrub;
Cape Barren geese on the wing or strutting prehistorically; whiting in spangled shallows.

ancient rock formations; hundred-million-year-old fossils; the great unconformity.
Giddy, too, with everything I feel: the love, even the losses and hurts, which tell me,
harshly, I am alive – alive right now, on this scrap of severed land

pushed up from the sea floor, encircling ocean aglitter with sunlight.
How good that we evolved among these creatures, came down from trees
in a distant past, the way kangaroos did, and developed a sense of what is beautiful.

The mind wanders as the path does, up through open forest, snaking among stringybark,
hakea and native mountain pepper berries. It spirals with the white-bellied
sea eagle on thermals over limestone cliffs, rises into sunshine and blue air

till it becomes nothing, dissolved into atoms of everything else. The mind drifts
as this continent will, right up into the northern hemisphere, smashing into continents
and civilisations. Molten rock will rush upwards, again, new horizons of dolerite

thrusting into sky, eroding down, cracking with cold into polygonal columns.
And here is joy. Joy welling up through layers of sadness, the way Bishop and Clerk's
dolerite rose up through buckled sandstone, limestone – unstoppable, inevitable.

That dolerite teeters now in high columns, cracking my view of the Tasman Sea,
of Freycinet Peninsula, Schouten Island, Ile des Phoques. Everywhere is gleaming ocean.
Beyond that eastern horizon you will be hiking, too, striding your long-legged strides,

walking your way to a kind of calm, but one which surrounds calamity.
At dusk, the sky turns some painter's hue – cobalt, or phthalo blue. Venus is already there,
shining like a star, big enough to reflect in daylight. Other stars arrive so surreptitiously

I can't say if they're in the sky or in my eyes. I like to think you will be looking upwards,
too. You'll notice Venus. And soon you'll see the later stars come on like fiesta lights,
and the Milky Way stream across us both. No moon. How we loved our moons. But now,

so many have gone by without you. Perhaps, it was just our love's allotted time
in the world's unfolding. Something ordained, something transient. But unlike Bette Davis,
I will continue to ask for the moon, for the stars, for this one brief beautiful life.

Shifting sands

The sculptor builds a schooner out of sand;
crowds marvel at the way it stands upright,
its sails full for all the world as if fanned

by a great wind. He knows his stuff,
has gathered sand in quantities enough
to grasp its fluid ways, the bluff involved

in working with the very small,
that any moment his tall, tawny ship
may fall into a heap; it's this

that ties the crowd in thrall, and him.
Through a microscope he's seen these grains,
as individual as human faces, or stars,

never one the same, their odd chain-like behaviour
the kind he aspires to tame. He's seen Gyuto monks
with their vivid mandalas of sand:

minute chunks of graded colour form buddhas,
flowers, trees, animals, stars,
all linked within a circle, later swept up

and poured into a river, rejoining the cycle
of erosion, abrasion, suspension, deposition,
the trickle of grains like that in an hourglass

reminding us weeks, months, years will pass
and we will pass with them,
at last coming to rest like sand at a point bar

or the mouth of a rare wild river,
far from home, but home,
beneath our star.

Town

Everything is smaller: the cenotaph with its gilt;
tilting verandahs all down Gilbert Street;
Kenworthys' store that never had a sale;
the railway yard now grey nomad heaven —
campervans, folding chairs, bare bludgeoned feet.

They've taken up the train tracks, laid a memorial walk.
People jog in lycra past the Axeman's Hall of Fame,
something to recognise in everyone you meet,
the same and not the same. It's as if your old life never did end:
you expect to see school friends exactly as they were,

Margaret's little sister with her flame red hair.
For every store you have a history:
you know who worked there, where they went.
It hid inside you all along, this town.
You grow smaller, too, when you return; you fit

inside the girl who marched each Anzac dawn,
who lay on the riverbank with boys she hardly knew. You burned —
bridges, hearts; the start of everything right here.
There, the bank, your first job; there, where you fell in love.
You longed to be beauty queen at Henley on Mersey,

watched the woodchop, that sheen on muscled arms.
The shale road turns out to have an actual name,
the shale works still there, and the ruined factory
where your mother processed flax in the war;
others long gone: Ovaltine factory, cannery, pulp mill.

Secret places along the river beckon, rendezvous of old,
the cold taste of river water pungent in your mouth.
You learned here the walks of life and walked away,
but everyone returns to that town inside them.
How far would you go to reclaim it?

You buy black tights in the grocery store for something to do
and learn it will become a delicatessen,
this farming town in the island's bread-basket turning trendy.
All day, the farm hovers on your mind's horizon, a private paradise
gained and lost, the lover you never get over.

The trees your father's father planted have grown so tall
it's just a matter of time. What can any town give you now?
But there are old people who stop you, say you've got your mother's
eyes; you turn the next street corner before you cry.
Some – very old – think you *are* your mother.

lingua franca

¿in Old Norse *tunga*, old Hoch Deutsch *zunga*
Latin *lingua*, Greek *glóssa*, we already hear the yoke:
harsh north, soft south
we are multi-lingual in the one tongue

tongue in cheek we might draw a link
with the Sanskrit *lingam*
or any linguiform projection of flesh
which lingers and saunters over the body

this language is the frank one

a child sticks out his tongue and I laugh
a man does the same
I blush, feel shame

some days tongues are everywhere:
silent in my boots
or the Town Hall bell
the small tongues of pasta called *linguini*
the lingulate leaves of local trees

have you seen them in butchers' shops
and wondered how ours would look
stretched out on a plate

it can howl like the screech owl
loll like a mollusc

the cat sometimes has it
or it is tied up elsewhere

feel the shock of another tongue in your mouth

we speak our dialects, our argots
for richer or poorer

tongues have gone missing
or are taught in desperation
by the last speaker of the lingo:
words of epic poems
the names of plants
another way to say, *I love you*, almost lost

in cuneiform and linear B
alphabet ideograph syllabary
we try to pin language down
like a butterfly under glass

a cute monkey climbed up a circumflex
and fell to his grave?

In Spanish

My fingers learn all the parts of your body
in Spanish, tracing each name into your skin –
dedos del pie on toes,
muslo against your thigh,
vientre into your belly.
Homework has never been such fun.
In conversation, I use every verb for making love
and nouns become intense with pleasure.
I eschew the past or future perfect;
and focus on the present.
We are conjugating from singular to plural,
a juggle of personal pronouns,
I through *we*, to *they*.
I am a beginner.
The Tao suggests we stay this way,
maintain beginner's mind.
Is there a choice?
All my life I've wanted love in another tongue,
one which gave back cadences and questions,
one which kissed my life with soft syllables.
A Romance language was first choice
for what I had in mind,
the kind of love you can't take home to mother.
Venice would be a good setting,
but I've been there and it's sinking.
Perhaps the Alhambra
on one of those nights when the air is a caress
and the scent of orange blossom catches
in everybody's hair.
Does love said in another language count?

Spanish puts a question mark
at the beginning as well as the end,
bracketing everything in interrogatives,
preparing you for the end.
We exist between them:
the question is beautiful;
we don't desire an answer.

Ariadne speaks

I've been to Naxos (I went there with a lover);
a beautiful island, not a bad place to be marooned.
The women cared for me; I didn't find another.

What doesn't kill you makes you tougher;
isn't that what's sung in all the tunes?
I've been to Naxos; I went there with my lover.

I can't forget how he stroked my body with a feather,
the way we lay together, yes, like two spoons.
If only he knew he looked so like my father.

It wasn't the minotaur; he slayed his mother.
Sorry to burst the mythological balloon.
I've been to Naxos; I went there with my lover.

Outside the labyrinth, the red thread became my tether;
he never once thanked me for holding on.
Still, on Naxos, I declared I would never love another.

He never said he loved me; truth is what I'd rather.
He abandoned me on Naxos, the night of the harvest moon.
I've been back to Naxos with my new significant other.
I don't care if Theseus ever made it home.

A paean to bones

Cleaning out my son's bedroom
now he's grown to another life,
I find a children's book about the body.
It's all here, the blood and guts, the sex,
but I open at bones. Words run
round the page like a poem, a prayer:
mandible, maxilla, cranium, clavicle.
I think about his precious head squeezing
towards the world, fontanelles gnashing.
I remember it. He remembers it.
Genes remember things, too:
and his bones will grow as tall
as my grandfather's, my great uncles'.
Thank you, world, for having him.
Scapula, femur, ulna, radius, carpals,
metatarsals: all those years of holding hands;
the first sight of them on a screen:
small nubs on the end of larger nubs.
I think about all of my son's bones,
how small they once were, now how large.
To think that every baby born
holds that complex code which builds
a skeleton and everything that goes with it.
You can see why people believe in gods.
I don't. But I am paying attention,
and attention is like prayer.
The thing is, I love every square inch of him
in a way that I won't love anyone else, ever.
It's almost beyond what's allowed;
something shared with the women

of the world, the rich and poor, safe
and unsafe, on leaky boats with children
lost to the sea. All of them. Once,
the smallest bones inside my body
were the ossicles – incus, malleus, stapes –
in my son's ears. What strange creatures
we are, built from calcium, carbon,
keratin, as outlandish as zebras,
giraffes, or undersea creatures
now male, now female.
Nothing is truly strange in the world;
and *everything* is strange.
Even blood is made *inside* our bones,
calcium factories running themselves.
Walking upright was a grand idea
in almost every way, except for the lower vertebrae,
but single tungsten blades outstrip femur,
knee, ankle and foot. We are not perfect,
only the best that could be made of things
with what was to hand. What will change?
Don't think evolution has done with us yet.
The book wants me to play a game,
throw a dice to live or die.
I'm already playing it. And I'm not winning.
But the game. The game is really something.

Drowning

If you happen to fall overboard, the manual says, do not flail.
Flailing attracts sharks. Instead, remain calm, float, breathe.
You might tread a little water or float upon the surface.
You might wait with patience for rescue or a miracle:
a helicopter dropping down, a local in a spinning coracle.
You may begin to see visions, your life flash before your eyes;
this is where the swings and roundabouts cut you down to size.
The cold is seeping in now and no lifebuoy in sight.
Remember you share this plight with people the world over.
Is it the cold, or the loneliness in the middle of the unforgiving ocean?

The boat will not turn back now, may not have seen you fall;
all your sins and their atonement, in fact *life*, begin to pall.
Perhaps this, this nothingness, holds a deep appeal,
a quietude, acceptance, nothing, not one thing, left to feel.

Afterlife

The river tells a story

Mist rising from the farthest reaches of Otago Bay, remnant of an early morning
Bridgewater Jerry. I walk further to where the land gives out altogether

in a fringe of casuarinas and slabs of ancient sandstone.
Scattered she-oak cones and needles conjure churches – that subtle scent of incense

the tang of salt can't quite disguise. The mist, I notice, has been transformed
into droplets which cling impossibly to the very ends of needles on the trees.

It's no use holding on, I could say. I find metaphors everywhere, of course,
but that's not why I've come. It's for the quiet, and the quiet's solace.

I make my mind like the river: smooth. Today, the Derwent is a bolt of shantung silk,
charcoal and silver. Four teal ducks flutter down from their driftwood tree,

and settle on the water. They sail along, unzipping the river's silk dress in four places.
My mind unzips like this whenever I think about you. Which is still too often.

Loss: it sounds like something small and smooth, a pebble, say, to keep
in your pocket, a lozenge to hold on your tongue. It isn't.

We sailed in summer to this stretch of river; even then I knew you didn't love me.
It's a lot to ask for two people to make a pair, but the birds here have no trouble.

Today, it's two cormorants, close in to shore, semi-submerged. They dive
simultaneously and torpedo underwater, then surface a surprising space away.

One tries to dry his wings while still in the water, extending them
the way cormorants do on a rock point, or pontoon, then sinking back

into the river. It's the sort of doomed task I'm asking of myself:
to stop loving you. The landscape around me is construed from loss:

grains of sand separate from this sandstone slab even as I sit here;
the whole valley slowly carved from stone; rain leaching mineral salts from land,

delivering them out to sea. Loss and gain; I try to remember that.
Last week this stone slab had *Iloveyou* scratched in cursive,

no space between the words, breathless. Perhaps a couple were out for a picnic,
and he would propose on his knees. He'd proffer a ring,

take her for champagne at a cool bar by the water.
Or perhaps it was a woman writing, a woman like me, trying to put outside of her

the loss of love, when she still has love inside her. I thought it would take months
before those words were whisked away by wind and wave-wash;

it took mere days. The words have turned to sand.
Love is this ephemeral. The river has a story to tell me,

one which might point the way forward if I learn how to listen.
I once said if things didn't work out with you, I wouldn't try again.

But I don't want to recede from life's shore like a tide which never turns.
Perhaps it's time to make up a new story, start from the beginning

again, never knowing how things might, or might not, end. In front of me,
the four ducks lift splashily from the river, and fly fast towards the zinc works'

shaft of steam as if they've received urgent news and have somewhere they must be.
The cormorant couple cruise the peninsula's point,

blue-black bodies threading their bird-cursive into the river,
my finger under each word.

Afterlife

(Bowl with aquatic decoration; Egypt, 1550-1295 BCE)

Three and half thousand years in the world
and your four Nile fish are still

swimming their marsh bowl,
spinning its web of intrigue,

appeasing or pleasing the goddess Hathor,
Lady of Turquoise, who adored this blue,

vivid from copper in the mix and the fire.
They have seen the rise and set of so many suns,

and the death of the one who fashioned your faience form,
who plastered silica over the mould,

to create this delicate vessel for the dead.
You have outlived your maker by numberless years,

outlived the fears of those left behind,
outlived belief in a life beyond.

The fish swim clockwise,
tracing the sun, its endless round –

though the maker knew it was our world that moved –
the sun's faithful rise from the dead of night,

the expected set.
Lotus buds protrude from bodies and mouths,

a flower that heeds the sun
the way sunflowers do,

opening,
closing,

every day a rebirth.
The fish's mouths are full of young;

this is how they're protected from harm
till they enter the Otherworld.

Etched in black lines, thin and unwavering,
then blasted in a furnace of wood no longer found

anywhere near the Nile.
What of your temple?

Perhaps a drowned place
now the Nile is walled in,

the marshes no longer wet,
their people moved to higher ground.

What say the triangles inverted in space
about time past and loss of place?

Are they an hourglass,
sifting sands that creep ever closer

to the floodplain?
Are they doorway from here into there?

The needle's eye?
No camel to be seen.

Is it the balance of life and death,
of day and night, of what we've had

and what is left?
From a god's eye-view,

it's a pyramid.
The fish go on swimming around, around;

they don't hold their breath,
or utter a sound.

They've been swimming for centuries,
hoping to please, and the bowl comes to rest

in this place by the sea -
mouth, estuary, where the waters meet,

a feat of luck, of finding, and gentle hands.
How has life not broken you?

Your turquoise goes on shining,
pleasing the eye,

faience body delicate, tender,
a fragile structure which surely would sing

if I stroked your rim.
Up close I see the fine cracks:

long devotion will always take some toll.
You are as frail as the human vessel,

easily crushed, the loss sorely felt.
With food for the afterlife,

the loved would live on,
joining the throng of immortals.

Perhaps you brimmed with sedge plant,
and powerful hieroglyphs assumed hostile lives,

ate all your food offerings,
consumed your power.

Did the temple scribe forget to sever creatures in two,
cut the horns from the horned viper,

remove the eyes from birds?
Your maker's people

knew the power of divine words.
Were you filled with water

for that long journey over?
You may have been pure symbol:

a jewel-like blue pool of undying light
from the sun, moon and stars,

and that life-giving potion —
faith, and love.

Like all art, you weren't then you were,
something from nothing,

an idea to be held in the hand,
an idea of copper, ochre, quartz and lime,

your mouthbrooding fish
orbiting their turquoise world like moons,

immortality
in their mouths.

A labyrinth is not a maze

This is the first thing you need to know.
A maze is for losing yourself,
a labyrinth for finding yourself.
When Odysseus entered the labyrinth,
he had no intention of being lost.
Ariadne would hold the red thread
at any cost until he'd slain his demon.
Would he slay it? Did he?
Round the planet people traipse labyrinths
some ancient, some copied, some brand new;
there are walking holidays, retreats, meditations.
Perhaps it comes down to the act of walking;
that's what we are made for, kilometres per day,
bodies slowly built for standing tall,
freeing hands, all this making
grown from that change.
In the museum, I pace my labyrinth:
this is my going-round underground,
one eye out for the minotaur.
It is my cloisters, for deep thought,
for learning poems, for prayer.
The air changes with the crowd.
It must be like that in church:
the priest sniffing whether it's for show,
a hedging of bets,
or whether someone believes.

An art to everything

(after Carl Phillips)

There's an art
to everything: how
a double rainbow breaks
and juts from red city roofs
on the drive home from work,

travelling forwards with me,
intensifying by the moment,
like an absent painter's palette,
colours smudging down
in the raining air.

How that means Easter,
late this year,
after the clocks have fallen back,
when early mornings remain black
and twilights disappear.

There will be blackberries for jam,
and figs slowly turning purple,
barrel pumpkins in painterly hues
at Monday's Sorell market.
Our land's the same wilderness,

springing up in blackberry spurs
from the neighbour's block,
bursting into wattle yellows,

thistles I dig out.
Trees are quietly building
another year's growth-ring.

At the museum,
all the man-made things,
very old and very new,
the little *Leda and the Swan*
still coupling,
fine figurines from Upper Egypt.
It's been said that hieroglyphs
are boasts writ large,
each cartouche a banner:

the crypt doors where a king
is revered for killing
one hundred and two lions in twenty years.
The art of giving:
extravagant, as when Mark Antony

sent sixteen barges full of sand
to build a beach for Cleopatra
on her island near Turkey,
or modest, a bowl
of lemons from a backyard tree.

There's an art
to the way a lover
might say he's not happy any more.
To saying he never was.
An art to remaining quiet.

There's an art to everything, even endings:
take a leaf from the book
of Marina Abramovic and her lover,
who walked for ninety days
from opposite ends of the Great Wall of China

to embrace at the mid-point
and say goodbye. Or
take a leaf,
fallen in autumn,
crimson.

Lady Gwendoline

Lady Gwendoline roars along the Brooker.
I look out for her on Fridays.
Her cab is gold
and her two-load tray shining silver.
She's a giant linked piece of jewellery
and I want her.
She's slow to get moving at the lights;
languorous is how I think of it,
but when she rolls she really rolls;
the weight of ore she bears adds momentum.
She's unlike the other trucks I see these mornings
with their dust and rust.
Lady Gwendoline gleams,
brilliant in the winter morning sun.
She dazzles other drivers, too.
She could be an accident waiting to happen,
a femme fatale of the highway.
She pulls alongside
and I change lanes to get close.
When she takes her leave at the next exit
it's like one of those country songs about loss:
Lady Gwendoline done gone and stole
my heart with her 36 wheels.
On the car radio a man from my neck of the woods
talks of his song called,
The bogan lovesong.
And that's what this is:
a love song about a truck.
I think it's easier this way.

Lunch break at the museum

I take my lunch to the peninsula's farthest point,
lie on the Triassic sandstone shelf, and breathe.
Salt air loosens my lungs, my heart.
Today, three pelicans take pride of place on the river,

sailing about like galleons. They look bizarre,
but nothing is impractical in nature.
One of them tramples the river in long wet strides,
beating mighty wings, chest muscles working overtime.

He treads the bay's length before becoming airborne.
The big webbed feet fold back into undercarriage
as the bird passes, one metre above the water.
He rounds the point as if a hairpin bend on a road.

Those immense wings! I think of Icarus, angels.
The air now feels solid, like something you could walk on.
Next comes a glide phase which takes him out of sight
past the old jetty and the long stairs to the museum.

Three minutes later, the second bird follows; three minutes more,
the third, each flight pattern identical.
It's as if they're doing trials, training a young one
on precisely timed take-offs, and charted flight paths.

I have many questions. I keep thinking:
if a fly uses a hundred times more oxygen
when launching into flight, how much must a pelican use?
There are dab chicks, too, low in the water,

doing their abrupt dives from a floating stillness;
youngsters copy, comically bobbing up like rubber ducks in a bath.
A crowd of crested terns gain height; they stall, hover, dive, stall again.
I'm watching momentary mid-air calculations take angled shape before me,

terns turning themselves into both arrow and bow. Their wings beat furiously.
One is right in front of me, his eyes on a silver sliver below the surface.
He is working everything he knows of geometry and light, thrust and strike,
till he dives for one second, two, comes up and flies off with the fish in his beak.

Great egrets lift their long legs delicately and place them just so.
They strut to and fro, then freeze, their eyes low on the silver whiting.
It's like a ballet; or a ballet is like this. They will stab a fish with swift precision.
Their white is startling. Like freshly washed bed sheets

on a summer clothesline. How do they stay so clean on tidal mud flats?
And two black swans sail by with cygnets in tow: two, four, five.
They must have hatched a second brood in this extended summer,
nature ever the opportunist.

Two metres away, too inexperienced, or shy, to head into open water,
a lone young pied oyster catcher picks his way along the shore,
pecking at this and that. To his surprise, he catches a spider
running on the surface of the river, and doesn't know what to do.

He lets it go, changes his mind, tries again, swallows it.
He stares out to the flocks of other birds. Word has spread.
Seagulls have arrived and there's a fishing frenzy.
Perhaps he's just the odd one out, the observer:

someone has to be.
I'm watching these small secular miracles the whole of my lunch break,

watching life in close-up: sentience, the cycle of survival.
There is no art to match it, and that's the truth.

I may as well direct visitors down to this lacy bit of coast
and bid them watch. It all but tears your heart out,
to think that we are just like this, but not nearly as nice.
There have been dolphins, but not today,

our cousins taking a turn around the bay after a school of fish.
We might have stayed the same, and done less harm.
If it's true nothing can be loved at speed – that's what the cartoonist told me –
well, I'm loving all this as slowly as I can in half an hour.

I'm getting lost in it. Like visitors to the museum,
we must bear with getting lost to find our way.
The cartoonist also said, *Don't be too afraid of unhappiness.*
I'm doing my best.

I listen to the secret language of a sudden breeze through she-oaks,
and watch the way it rushes like a brush across the water,
ruffling a feather here and there. There's a subtle soft addition
to the cushion layer of she-oak needles and a scent of incense

as they cleave. Water breaks against the shore in lines of poetry, or prayer.
It's like visiting a Shinto shrine: something speaks to you
but not in ways you can decipher.
Love of the world has entered through your skin.

If I thought there was divine design, then an estuarine mud flat
would be one place to find it. In the museum, the grandest work
is nature's, a twenty-metre slice down to this same sandstone
showing us, layer by layer, how young we are.

I sit stunned by stone-time and the age of the sun.
Sometimes I wish we didn't strive to understand more,
just go back to the old stories. It's the push-pull of knowledge, isn't it.
You want it, but you don't. I want to know what these birds know.

Soon, I'll run back to the museum to look after things
humans think important, but every minute here helps.
This might be mere survival but it looks like joy.
And some other species, observing me, might think the same.

Porcelain dreams

China China – Bust 1982 porcelain
by Ah Xian

Tree branches clutch at his throat,
and pavilions nestle in the dip of clavicle;
people drink tea or make love there.
Dreams play over eyelids closed
beneath the soar of mountains,
and narrow paths cling to the sheer side of his cranium.
There are abrupt pagodas
and peaks receding, losing themselves in mist.
Sampans ply from shoulder blade to shore,
ferrying loved ones to those who wait with outstretched arms.
He is dreaming Ming dreams in blue on white
and his many brothers, fired in the same kiln,
also carry their home and culture
like a tattoo into the world.
His flawless porcelain skin is translucent,
the passing light so like the light of life
you want to wake him up
and tell him what you've seen.
Our own bodies are marked:
history imprinted visibly, invisibly.
We may as well be the tattooed skin
stretched in a display cabinet,
people tracing their fingers over our past:
it's all written on the body.
And in another cabinet, dark glass
reflects his gleaming figure,
a single gold coin drifting in the black above him,
a newly risen moon
in the black sky of his dreaming.

Larnax with octopus

(Crete, Late Minoan c.1325 – 1275 BCE)

This larnax was unearthed
as if birthed from the past,
its foetal body a layer of dust –
lust, love, loss, longing all come to an end,
a mend in the tear of life's fabric.
We could tell who you were
and who were your kin
with a little string of letters
from a scrap of bone.
But you knew your family,
and your foes, those who'd kiss
or kill you. This was the essential
thing to know. But the flow
of weather, too, you'd learn,
so that one look at a stern sky
could decide the harvest or the hay;
the way birds returned
early, or leaves unfurled late,
could say the fate of toil.
Oil from that year's olives
spoke a story of the rain,
and ordained your future.
One foot on land, one on sea,
duties changing with the season:
farmer, fisher, warrior.
Were you a farmer
who went to sea, or fisher
who stayed home? Your wife alone
in the house when you were gone,

the nights long.
Her thoughts would turn
to widowing waves, the sea's
sneaky ways of picking over men's bones.
Respect for the ocean, her creatures
and bounty, meant fiestas for her spirit.
And each larnax was adorned with beasts
of the sea; the clever octopus
your wife's choice, her voice
following you into the next life.

Long lonesome man

Lange Eenzame Man 2010
by Berlinde De Bruyckere

1.

Those eloquent buttocks;
he could be sleeping.
Someone with pale, pasty skin,
someone who stays indoors too much,
probably drinking.
Beyond the narrow hips and lean thighs,
patellas jutting forwards,
delicate ankles,
and the topography of tendons,
it's those feet I'm drawn to again and again.
On one heel the bone seems to break through
too much line-dancing perhaps,
or a mother who polished that irresistible heel
in the palm of her hand a little too long,
more than was seemly.
Long, pale soles rippled like sand,
flattened pads beneath the hammer toes:
the smallest toe grub-like and vulnerable.
I like to think of him taking long walks,
striding paths in the bush, empty beaches
and the streets of sunlit cities.
Yes, they remind me of feet I have loved,
sensitive soles that I miss.
I hope these feet have often been kissed.
I want to kiss them myself.

2.

Where is the adamant angle of elbow?
Where are tarsals, and metatarsals?
There was no one to hug,
so the arms have gone.
No head, no arms,
minus fingerprints or face —
he is anonymous, alone.
Nothing to make him different from any other man.
And yet we *are* our bodies:
everything about him is here, somewhere,
what he has loved, endured,
the many acts this body has made,
acts of love and compassion, or of hatred.
Something here makes us feel for all men,
anyman, everyman,
a length of bone and blood,
meat and muscle,
disintegrating, decaying,
alone at the end but not lonely,
no longing,
nothing.

3.

We are flesh:
who we are is written on our body.
Why is it not here to see?
Do we need palaeontologists
working out the wear on teeth,
the cellular construction of bones,
the precise shape of brain cavity?
He is simply one in a long line
of homo sapiens,
walking tall for longer than we originally thought,
for six million years,
standing up even in the trees,
adapting to rapid change,
drought, flood, drought,
forest, desert, ice.
He is an example of a species,
a man among men,
a someone then,
and now the model
for a headless torso in a museum.

Second day of spring

If you sit here long enough you begin to know
what the river is saying about impermanence.
You start to think of the tinkling lap of water against stone
as the only music that will last. You hear wind

in the she-oaks as one long out-breath, then one in-breath,
as if everything is meditating on the end of winter,
the beginning of spring.
On the far shore, cherry trees are in pink blossom.

Already, pale petals float across the bay like confetti
from a recent wedding. I think of Pablo Neruda:
I want to do with you what spring does with the cherry trees.
But the sun on my bare skin is as close even to kissing

as I'll get. I don't mind that now there's no one
with me, savouring the silver, silken river;
this place makes aloneness pleasure.
Birds keep me company:

twelve hoary-headed grebes, and a flotilla of Eurasian coots,
which dive for fifteen seconds at a time.
I count, holding my breath too,
waiting for each featherweight body to pop up again.

Two black swans sail past as if life is this easy,
yet with something funereal in the mourning satin
of that fancy froth of feathers,
and eyes red as if from crying.

Four teal ducks swim right up to my naked feet
and chitter as they feed on something green;
I'd love to know what they say about a day like this,
and if they have any sense that days are numbered.

I know spring is stirring in them, but how does it feel?
It's impossible to hold in mind the long length of time
it's taken to have all this life, here, today: the Now is so big.
I am in it. They are in it. Today, that is enough.

The girl with her hair towards heaven

(in *Theatre of the World* exhibition)

Imagine this: in one room
arranged in semi-circular rows
is all the world's knowledge.

If I stand at mid-centre front,
my view is what mankind has made
of itself with what has been given.

What did we arrive with? This awkward
spine, straightened by circumstance,
weakened by millennia of four-footedness.

Eyes. Some say the eyes have it:
responsible for the Cambrian explosion
and everything that followed. Us.

Prehensile hands. Everything we've done,
done with these hands. Freed of walking,
they built and sowed, killed and mowed.

Oh man! Man! That big brain, in its silly sack.
Skull thick; never thick enough:
spilled brains throughout history.

And up there, fifth from the right,
third from the top is the girl with her hair
towards heaven. She reminds me of our fall

from our highest aspiration: humanity.
Greed, I suppose, is what did it.
Always, always, wanting more.

The peach orchard of immortality

Geode in the shape of peach inscribed with Chinese writing

1.

Chalcedony: the sound
a round pebble in your mouth.
You want to lick its smooth flank.
You want to cradle it between your hands,
like a bird, a chalice, a small earth kept safe.
To me, it is a weighty heart,
wrenched from the ribs of earth,
somewhere in the Turtle Mountains,
long before the round of death and birth on land.
A mix of nature and culture,
it is about living to grow old,
but tells us how young we are
in the scheme of things.

2.

I've seen such geodes at Salamanca market,
cracked open like stone eggs
to their amethyst lining.
There is water at your centre – 240 million years old.
What could this water tell us about that time?
That water became less hospitable?
That fish began to heave themselves onto land,
grow lungs, and bones in their fins.
That hands began, a change amazing
as the Cambrian explosion,
at least for us, since hands have made us
who we are: artisans.
Whose hands, in history, have held you?

3.

In the Peach Orchard of Immortality,
trees took three thousand years to ripen.
Time itself was slowed:
petty human time counted for nothing.
Some revered artisan in China
was handed this geode
to turn it into an artefact,
a plea for longevity.
We all want more life.
But does a sense of an afterlife, however vague,
stop us living the now?
We are like pharaohs who spent their reign
building tombs, preparing for the long hereafter.

Rowing down the Nile

A woman is rowing down the Nile alone,
because she wants to, and she can.

The boat is old, but it is *her* boat,
and she trusts it. The oars are heavy;

the sides are painted with gaudy stars;
there are ropes instead of rowlocks

and, inside, the bottom grows fake grass.
She has become wily

and wears the garb of a boatman;
white robes hide her figure and her face.

But no one is expecting to see a woman
rowing down the Nile, no one's heard of such a thing.

There is fear,
but she is following her feelings, not her fears.

The rhythm of rowing soothes her,
the warm air flows by her,

and all the life of the river becomes part
of her present and past.

She can't know what the future holds till it arrives.
She passes islands, boats full of sedge grass, stone ruins,

date palms, farmers, temples, stands of papyrus, ibis.
Feluccas float by, and cruise ships.

A Pied King Fisher hovers near her,
poised to dive for its prey.

Now and then, she looks for crocodiles.
At night she anchors by the lee shore;

her palms are raw,
and the backs of her hands and tops of her feet

burn from the endless sun.
Her arms and body ache.

But she is so happy.
Sometimes she goes ashore and builds a small fire,

for company, a tiny red glow on the edge of the desert.
Then she lies down in the bottom of her boat

and gazes at the night sky.
Every one of the two and a half thousand stars

visible to the human eye, she can see.
She is gliding along the milky way,

floating out into the universe.
If she never does one other thing in her life,

it won't matter.
She listens to river water lapping on the hull

and dreams of what this river knows:
its finest self ascending mountain air;

falling, gushing, teeming;
spreading smooth and placid in lakes;

spinning rainbows as it thunders thousands of metres,
down, down;

its crocodiles growing fat on fish knocked senseless
by the smash of water;

birds thrilling to the bounty,
taking to the air.

And then, the greenish brown Blue Nile
joins the greyish brown White Nile

in *the longest kiss in history,*
the long confluence

proceeding for kilometres before their waters truly mingle
to become this Nile on which she sleeps,

and rows. From Luxor to Qena she rows.
Then she leaves her boat by the side of the river

for someone else to find, and be happy.
And not one of her fears has come to pass.

Vapour trails

Vapour trails

And vapour trails are dividing up the sky the way fences
  make geometry of farms, air force jets hurtling through
    that hurtful blue, heading for their practice mountains.
      Even out of sight, Bass Strait glitters; you feel it in the light

when you look up. Those pilots with their aerial view
  absorb everything I saw driving: paddock reds and greens,
    glinting dams, Narawntapu to the east, Mt Roland
      to the west, childhood landmarks barely understood.

It's as if a needle has taken thread from the spool of white
  cloud and is sewing up the blue, stringing clouds together
    as we once threaded shells at Hawley Beach on strands of catgut.
      The sky's become a chalkboard for hieroglyphs, writ large

but untranslated. I drive down Bonney's Lane, Armitage Lane.
  Linear irrigators crawl up hillsides, gargantuan stick insects
    on every horizon, like some robotic army taking over the coast,
      their pivots making crop circles the fighter pilots admire,

easing through gapped fences and crushing their way through crops.
  Wind turbines are whirling this place into the future:
    our old farm has gone organic, and crowds of backpackers
      do the job of herbicides. Who knows what future

I might have had here? But life rolls on like those irrigators,
  set in motion by instructions from some invisible hand,
    or perhaps a sort of SIM card hidden in the land, or deep inside us.
      Then there's that fat, full moon rising through the horizon's

pinkish haze, as we laze around the outdoor table drinking wine.
I feel its gravity on my bones, a pull on eyes, my hands.
I would reach out and touch it, that grand rock reminding us
of our minute niche in the scheme of things. It's the same

with this place, its pull on my body waning, waxing, skin
responding. When I walked over the land above Moorlands beach,
I knew its bones. My past lived here. I watched planes manoeuvre
to land at Pardoe drome. I know what that's like: barely

over the coast and then you're home. It still brings me to tears.
I remember when, as a child, I thought some of our visitors
lived in the sky. We'd drive them to this airport and I would dream
of their eyrie life in the clouds. Further on, by chance,

in the little Northdown churchyard, I find my great-grandfather
with my great-grandmother, sharing a grave the way
they share my history, now part of the iron-rich earth.
The next morning, the full moon follows me out of town;

she's been up all night, and now rides the hills to my right,
sometimes getting ahead of me, sometimes holding back,
like a shining child running after my car; like my heart.
Past The Big Spud and all the farm names I used to know,

that silver disc in my mind and then my rear-view mirror,
as dawn turns the sky above Sassafras rose-coloured.
I pass trees quietly growing, dairy cows breathing out steam;
the Western Tiers startle up, red, from the green valleys,

and the sun rises like a dream lover over my horizon. The moon
  says goodbye. But that night, when I drive onward to where I live,
    the moon looms up once more. I can see why she's called *she*:
      wearing the lacy cloud archly, like a veil. She's been all the way

around the world and back again, the same, but different, every time.
  You have to feel awe for the way everything holds together –
    that moon, this Earth, the sun, the other stars, all the space between –
      and the way sea, air, earth and sunshine can ever feel like home.

Boy learning to juggle with lemons

For Sarah

He begins with two, as instructed.
Up and over the invisible wall
that stretches from him to me.

One two, one...two, onetwo, one two,
like marching girls, or boy soldiers
unsure of their footing.

His little brain seethes, cerebellum
so happy in this new act, something
to get its teeth into. One two, one two.

He's cocky, this fifteen year old,
adds a third ball and drops it.
But, not fazed by failure,

he marries three spinning spheres
in a flurry of physics and human adaptation.
The sunlit air builds a new structure:

curved lines like those of spinning atoms
careen around the fig tree, the lemon,
the pomegranate. Soon they lie like skeins

of memory round my garden.
And he is so happy with his new skill;
he wants to show his girlfriend,

impress her, make her laugh. He wants
to teach her, too, the way my friend's
daughter taught me, invisible threads

stretching across towns, states, countries,
connecting us better than phones,
no matter how smart. Soon, it will be cars,

ever bigger motor skills,
cerebellum aiming for automation.
He will be whirling into the future,

down that long unpredictable road,
so many balls in the air
and not even caring.

Earthing

It's as if they've landed here,
fallen from the blue sky, like Icarus.
They feel no brokenness, only something electric;
perhaps electrons in their bodies charged
as they passed through space.

Or is it the firing of neurons,
transmission synapse to synapse,
a festival of electro-chemical events?
Molecular messages pass to and fro,
to and fro, and what can decipher them?

The breeze? Cold sunshine? Glassy air?
Hillsides tip drunkenly beneath them.
It's like a Brett Whiteley painting, she says:
green and gold folds of land,
country lanes curling in and out of view,

birds and nests and eggs suddenly symbolic,
symphonic. Perspective is lost, then gained.
She's been confusing land and landscape,
searching for the sublime,
and had missed that third dimension,

the one they lie in, full tilt, flat out,
spreadeagled in wet grass,
laying down electric song-lines,
short-circuiting resistance.
Bush parrots fossick among the wild grasses;

they watch for the birds to lift away
in a burst of colour, of life, as they might do
themselves, and fly right back up to the sun.
Anything is possible.
And in the metre beneath them,

insects, mites, microscopic organisms;
the layer where the difference between life
and non-life is minor: a few cells, a beating core.
And then the lifeless spaces
stretching towards a scalding centre,

reminder of beginnings and endings,
the unlikely event of life on earth.
At that solid core beyond the molten, their bodies meet,
geometric trajectories of heat and light and love.
What a playful outcome are humans.

The sun and a glimpse of blue bay keep them in their place –
this valley, this swale, a single fold in earth and time.
It's a wild ride, life. Dig and plant and sow.
And the trees will grow, and the garlic, and peas.
But in the end, it's what you know about who you are.

They have waited and watched this land, learned its secrets:
how the water pools, where the wallabies sleep,
what the soil desires, the sun's seasoned pathways.
If there is anything they love about themselves,
it's right here.

Kunanyi

Kunanyi wakes me, writing her name in my hands
on the soles of my feet,
making her presence felt.
From my bed-cocoon I feel her precise shape
to the west: I look to her for permission, for weather,
for time. Time is what she holds in her heart,
millions of years of it.

Between the blood moons,
everything is in transition.
The one we saw over the mountain
transfixed our eyes.
Eyes full of mountain.
Hands full of mountain.

In the book I'm reading, the boy
who sees into the future says
the birds will all die.
He means, die out.
Birds flirt with the mountain,
hiding, singing, playing, soaring.
They love her, too.

Out to Sphinx Rock, the Upper Sawmill Track,
south below the Organ Pipes and up the Zigzag Track.
At every hairpin bend our view expands:
today, Bishop and Clarke on Maria Island
and, further north, The Hazards.
The land is showing its age:
soft folds of hills so dear.

The river is a gleaming blade
of some soft precious metal,
and the sky inexplicable, despite physics.

Thirteen ways of looking at a platypus

(after Wallace Stevens)

1.

Beyond hills the Chinese mined,
a small lake at sunset, a V-shaped interruption
to our thoughts.

2.

In tidy town, the platypus is king.
This is the treasure quiet can bring.
Wait, only breathing.

3.

At Cascade Reserve, three platypuses;
mother, father, baby.
This is what we suppose.

4.

Two years later, they are back:
same parents, different offspring?
Different family? We are not we any more.

5.

This is myth made real.
Duck plus what?
People can't believe what they haven't seen.

6.

One is lost, crossing a highway.
The call goes out and volunteer lovers of wildlife
leap to help.

7.
No one has ever seen a platypus have sex.
If only a platypus knew to savour this privacy,
it would.

8.
Monotreme. One hole.
We know what that means.
And don't. Basho would know what to make of it.

9.
The platypus pushes us to the edge.
At Cambridge in the river we guessed 'rat'.
Wherever you go, there you are.

10.
What does a platypus think about?
Water, water, food, food, sex, sex,
swim, swim.

11.
Like a thought almost caught,
that sight in the corner of the eye.
But was it?

12.
More at home than us in this world.
If a platypus could laugh,
it would.

13.
I do not know which to prefer:
seeing a platypus,
or hoping to see one.

Musicophilia

for Rowan

You tell me there are gods
who walk amongst us.
I remind you of false idols;
surely the nuns and brothers warned you.
You remain speechless:
you have witnessed the miracle
and now you will try to understand
or to accept mystery.
You add silence to your monkish life.
Thousands gather to worship:
they have come from round the country,
pilgrims ecstatic in the presence of holiness.
The crowd passes bodies of the faithful
above heads, hand to hand towards the saviour.
And he, a simple man with a Kiwi accent,
has somehow reached inside each worshipper,
found that string of life and made it sing.
Music: one of life's grand mysteries,
like language, like love,
constructed, perhaps, to fill the void.
But how did two brothers in a backwater garage
reach inside themselves and find this key to your universe?
How did they pull sound from their homemade guitars,
work larynxes in ways godlike,
find words that had always been aligned?
How did they turn nothing
into many somethings?
In the beginning was the word,
and that word and that melody

and that refrain, that plangent chord,
that unexpected run of notes,
the awaited return.
How did they draw out of the ether
things nobody knew they needed,
but then they did?
They understood this need for something –
what is it – beauty? Is it orgasmic,
cataclysmic, fantastic. Is it human?
How did these assemblages of carbon
find things not clearly constructed by evolution.
I mean, what is music for?
Okay, it's clear a good song will get you laid –
ask the Beatles, or Nick Cave –
but is that all? A good song
will carry you humming through the day;
lyrics undo you and make you up again.
When did we learn this?
And why do some learn it more than others?
Musicophilia is something everybody knows.
The birds know it: listen to the butcher bird,
the magpie warbling out its song.
We have so much in common.
Now they reach inside others and pluck
strings there, vibrating souls, bodies.
It has everything religion requires:
devotion, miracles, communion,
confession, absolution.
It might even save you.

Quicksand

We all know about quicksand, right?
One moment you're strolling along, whistling,
or maybe singing a song by K.D. Laing,
then bang! you're up to your neck.
Moments and moments pile up on themselves
and time begins to bend,
as a small voice starts up in your mind,
This is the end! That's it! It's over!
As the shock ebbs, you look about.
Everything looks familiar and safe out there:
no danger signs; nothing
to distinguish this patch of ground
from that around it.
Yet some niggling voice tells you,
You weren't alert. You were too relaxed!
And you know it's true.
You think about your body, now crushed,
think of all the wounds, the knives,
the hushed theatre where your life hung by a thread.
The last wound has barely healed. Such a shame
that now there's only your head.
And your head is mad, mad, mad.
Heat exhaustion, thirst, starvation await;
birds will peck out your eyes; soon or late
ants will move into your mouth.
You think about the man, stuck in stone,
who severed his arm to save his life.
But all you have is your head.
You take stock: stay and die, or try.
For a second or two you consider doing nothing;

how sweet the nothing would be,
but you have always wanted to be free
and this is the opposite.
It will be hard, it will take time,
and you will have to draw on every single thing you know.
But you begin:
you wriggle a toe.

The beach

after Robert Hass *Happiness*

Because the sun was gone behind the mountain's sleeping black-bull back
(though of course it was the mountain that moved)
and the sky was a page from the cloud atlas –
high cirrus or mares' tales, patches of mackerel –
so that above the city was splashed pomegranate pink
that shifted hue to mandarin, then peach,
and some clouds had stretched themselves above the black into straight lit-up lines

and because a jet aeroplane was distantly arriving
leaving a silver vapour trail ascending into the paintbox sky
and there was no wind and the river was the inside of an abalone shell
painting the beach silver as it lapped
and the brand-new sandstone wall was glowing rose in the golden light

and because my big son was off doing front-flips, somersaults and shoulder rolls
among the tussocky shining sand dunes then loping back to tell me
then loping off again and not needing me

and because people with poodles and Dalmatians, kelpies and border collies,
golden retrievers and whippets were walking very fast and throwing balls
with those whippy rubber ball-throwers and joggers jogged by in shimmering lycra

and the moon was a sixpence cut in half and the ceramic owl on the pier boatshed
was staring across to Droughty Point perhaps waiting for the next full moon to rise there
and roll out its silver carpet across the darkening Derwent

I decided to stand still,
and when I stood still
time itself seemed to stop and wait with me
for what would happen next.

The comfort of cows

Cows are never bored:
they always have something to do
even if it doesn't look that way.
They ruminate constantly,
even while watching you watching them.
Cows are warm. Seriously, if you are cold,
get close to a cow.
Cows are curious:
they will always stop what they are doing
to watch what you are doing.

We are cruel to cows:
we steal their babies year after year.
They grieve.
Cows prefer company:
eight is a good herd.
They know there's safety in numbers,
and cows can count.
Cows do not have eyes in the back of their heads
but they do have eyes in the side of their heads;
they can see trouble coming
better than us.
Cows know other cows
just like we know other people;
which ones to trust, who to avoid.
They know who is good to lick,
who to horn in the shoulder.
Cows love jazz:
they will moo their love the whole time.

Cows are content,

chewing cud, ruminating, thinking about other cows,

thinking about grass.

Farmers know almost everything their cows say:

time to milk me;

where's my food;

I'm scared of this crack in the ground;

why did you take away my baby?

Cows can be sad; they get scared; they feel pain.

Cows are exactly like us, except they have nicer eyes.

Cows can be dangerous: don't let one sit on you,

or stand on your foot; and don't stand too close to their tail.

Cow pats make excellent Frisbees

and are also good on your garden.

Eight thousand years of keeping cows

and only now do we wonder what they think about.

Cows are our friends.

I miss cows.

If there were cows in the city

we would all be happier.

But the cows would hate it.

The marvellous tree

I know your names:
one in the dead language of Linnaeus,
one a common name: yellow ash.
You are, like most things, paradoxical.
But you know nothing of the names we make for you.
To me, you are old friend,

encountered after years, embraced,
your yellowness a wide smile of welcome.
Remember me!
I'm wearing the same yellow coat!
It is a glorious coat: vivid, vibrant,
a shock of yellow glowing by the Koonya roadside,

beaming at drivers, at children.
Look at me! It's autumn!
All these years you've stood,
doing no harm, steadfast, calm.
Your girth has thickened and you're taller
but, in some intrinsic way, unchanged.

I remember, years ago, standing inside your yellow bounty,
leaves jinking like butterflies in the breeze,
time drifting about my ears.
Since then, I've learned what makes you yellow,
and what makes your leaves fall.
But science isn't everything.

Nor is the mathematics I'm told is there:
fractals forming with each push of new cells,

dendritic branching to a peculiar set of instructions.
There may be something as abstract
as the Mandelbrot Set inside you,
but beauty also resides there.

One part of my brain sings yellow;
one part whispers leaf-shaped;
yet another lets your leaves shiver in the wind.
My brainwaves make the whole
and I am glad of this, ever thankful
brain and body have grown and learned

so well they can perceive you;
eyes to see, hands to touch, ears to hear –
evolutionary marvels.
I listen for the moment of parting, of *leaving*;
you are, leaf by leaf, becoming your new self,
ending one journey, beginning another.

You will wait now, through the cold months,
keeping yourself to yourself.
But quietly, each day when the sun is out, you will work.
You may also be humming.
There is something serene in being near you;
I want your light, your stillness, your complicated beauty.

I lie in the damp grass and pull yellow over me;
it's like a forest burial, or an estivation.
I am slowing myself down: heartbeat, breath,
waiting for my next season.
Do trees ever feel lonely? I'd think, yes,
that you would long for the chemical conversations,

your roots mingling with others',
friendly vying for that special angle of sunlight.
Anyway, you have company:
black swans fly over you towards Norfolk bay,
pairs of oyster catchers too;
wombats and wallabies pass beneath you.

Young Hereford cattle low to you across the highway.
Rosehips shine back at you.
Don't be lonely: we are all kin,
for this is how the world was made.
But, probably, the answer is no,
you don't stand proud, or lonely,

or wishing things otherwise;
you simply stand.
Life washes through you:
you have sent seeds into the world,
roots into the earth,
you are strong.

In solitude, you are yourself.
Tides slip sheets of still water
to and from the sandstone coast;
years pass, and still you stand.
You stand some more.
You live.

Beginnings and endings

She always wanted happy endings,
but just got endings.
Her order form was surely incorrect:
they make those boxes you tick so small!
She's happy, though, to have been invited to the ball.
And she was thankful to have a dance partner,
never mind dance with a prince.
There was that night in Bali
when a frog landed on her pillow.
He was certainly green and charming
but she said, You must be in the wrong story,
and put him outside by a pond.

She can't live in the city now
where people move so fast.
She's returned to childhood:
staying outside with the other animals
and never watching the news.
She could never tell, anyway,
who was good and who was bad;
and the news makes everybody sad.
No one explained life would grow so complex.
She remains confused: no matter how she tries
she can't grasp quantum physics,
the cosmos or the nature of time.

She's been stitched up, had one with the lot,
but she's given it her best shot.
She's glad to have had a beginning at all:
one microscopic cell wriggling into another,

the way they say it all began,
the life explosion, that is, not the Big Bang,
that grand Beginning that goes on and on,
like a song you can't get out of your head.
On her best days, she writes a new poem,
or laughs and hugs her son;
there's no telling how they'll turn out
but she's glad to have begun.

Trick of light

The painter

i.m. Max Angus

Here is the painter, at ninety-nine, who goes out painting
en plein air every Sunday morning. Here's his wife,
whose shoe fell off like Cinderella's at his last exhibition;
someone helped, and held it out for her, a glass slipper.
They sat then, royalty, he on his chair in a vivid red vest,
like a flame robin, and she in her wheeled chair,
his princess. It was almost painful to see their love,
as thick as the paint on canvases, as bright in their eyes
as those colours, or the spots of light in the eyes of their birds.
They seem to know what birds know: how to sit in the bush;
where they are; *what* they are. How not to think, simply to be.
They know how to store up treasure inside themselves,
feeling rich every day, and how to give it back to us,
so we feel rich too.

Arrows

The sky is full of arrows, swish and whistle
of wing scythe. It is an onslaught of air,
a frantic weaving of flightpaths, their stitch
stiff wingbeats of coal-feathered shearwaters
home from the sea. They shatter the dusk.
Hatchlings trill a welcome as parents fat
with fish crash into dune-sand, bumble
through scrub. In black burrow mouths,
their gaping beaks regurgitate the day's
mashed catch with wheezy gasps and squeals.
Dune grass moves with sooty shapes
which missed their mark by a metre or so.
We imagine dark rafts of these birds
patching the ocean south of here,
their dawn-to-dusk hunt for food.
We wonder what they feel and what
they think as they fly the fracas of this daily
homecoming; we imagine one bird's
consciousness among thousands
of hurtling bodies. Mathematicians
believe they know how it's done,
but how does it *feel?*
The sea shivers into shore below us
in long ghostly verticals.
The surfers have all gone home now
to that city beyond this ring of hills.
A bushfire pall drifts south
towards us, veiling the stars
which cluster and brighten against
the deepening black. Dusk, then night,

and still they come, purposeful, diligent,
flung at the coast by the same internal algebra,
and unseen heavenly hexagrams,
which fly them across the globe,
and back again next summer
to this same jut of land, the same burrow.
What I would give for such sure instincts
of home and brood, of love and purpose.
But, you and I are sprawled together
on these tussocky dunes, with the Milky Way
soaring over us, and meteors falling
away to nothing. In places like this,
uncertainty can fall away to nothing, too.
Call it what you will: biophilia;
instinct; some might call it god.

The women

The women stand facing stone, arms akimbo,
as if it's their private wailing wall.
I see snatches of green flash from vine to bag.
Their fingers will be stroking each leaf like a child's hand,
testing for tenderness, the raised veins a braille of growth,
read by years of experience, without thought.
Thoughts are elsewhere, driving the talk.
They will gather in Toula's kitchen,
efficient as a production line of factory workers,
assembling pine nuts and rice, olive oil and lemon,
their chatter breaking like waves on the kitchen walls.
They will wrap parcels of sunlight and time
tight as cigars, into palmfuls of love,
the knowledge, like knitting or playing piano,
stored in their fingers.
Later, they will bite the resistant young skins;
oil will polish their lips.
They remember this making, this tasting,
waiting for men to come home from the sea.
How they would wrap five for luck
in a square of linen and run to the port,
hoping, hoping.

This is what life does.

after Eleanor Lerman

This is what life does.
Life lets you get up from your writing
and drive to the beach. It lets you see
the glitter growing smaller all the way
to the horizon. It lets you sit at a café
and order a latte with amber honey
in a little dish and watch all the people
walk up and down the beach,
some with ice-creams, some with dogs.
Life lets you join them. Life lets you take
off your shoes and push your toes deep
into soft hot sand.
Life doesn't care if sand gets in your car
or in your bed or in your navel.
Life lets some of the people do tai-chi,
others throw balls to their dogs
and if you stick around till nightfall
you'll see that Life lets other things
happen to young men and young women.
Do you have to be young to do those things?
you ask Life, but Life hasn't answered yet.
And when you were young you hardly
noticed that Life let you do anything.
You thought it was you who let you do things.
But Life lets you do everything you do.
Life lets you give praise for words like *pluvial*
whose meaning hovers at the edge of your mind,
almost raining.
Life lets you give thanks to the lover

who gave you the big fat dictionary
in which you'll look up the word.
It lets you play the guitar he gave you.
Life lets you think.
Life lets you kiss friends hello on each cheek
as if you were in France.
Life lets you hug your son who's grown
bigger than your own body,
which once held him inside it.
Life lets you drink a glass of cold wine
under the grapevine in your garden
as the sun sets behind the mountain.
Life lets you imagine the vivid red
of the waratah in bloom
on your favourite walk and taste
the beaded nectar caught among the red
even when you're not there.
Life lets you breathe in the ocean air
and wake up your heart which has been
in a coma since its accident in love.
Life lets you know that you are lucky.
Lucky to be here. Lucky to be here still. Lucky.
Not brave, not clever, not even interesting,
but alive. Lucky to be alive.
I've just been lucky.

tree conversations

after e.e. cummings

tree by leaf they speak their green
their words not heard nor ever seen
their lusts are said in ways unknown
to us or them as they are grown

branch by twig they vent their sap
stone by earth they build their map
birds know how to speak with trees
butterflies do and so do bees

root by root they speak to earth
from twig to branch to trunk of girth
the bark the heart the widening rings
the growing song that each tree sings

atom by atom they take the air
gobble it up and make it theirs
they use its carbon building blocks
their architecture really rocks

drop by drop they drink the rain
ring by ring they grow their grain
their every day brims with birth
keeping alive this little Earth

Trick of light

A sickle moon is pinning up the black sky,
looming larger as we drive each block on Harrington Street,
past St Mary's cathedral and onto the strip.
We're nervous: we've forgotten how to be hip.

The limpid yellow liquid that swirls around my glass
has wound its way into my veins like love,
a swoon, addiction, absolver of pain.
Let fall that mother mantle, suited but anonymous
and welcome bare shoulders glimpsed from a darkened bus
as if off to the most exciting evening.
And who's to say this is not the truth?

And now that night is done with its anti-climax,
I could spend my days writing out the facts,
but facts, you must know, will not be still like cells under a microscope
and even their accumulation will not restore the hope.
What happened to that restless girl, the one you knew best?
Did her dreams come down to earth? Did she dress as someone else,
lose her boots, and not get home?

I've learned that if you look away from things – it's a trick of light – they shift,
that life is full of fog and mist and spindrift,
that even clouds are far, far different than they look,
and that it never pays to do things by the book.
The girl has in fact never gone away, just hidden
herself inside another self, layer after layer
like a midden in a sand dune, or a babushka doll.
She's still there with her long hair and straight back
astride a horse – no disappointments, no hurts, no remorse.

She's still there on her first day at school, all those rules,
and the boys who chased her round the yard.

Up in your loft the rain started and didn't stop
as if the earth had found a new source of water.
I believe the sky was crying for the mother of the daughter
whose father threw her from a bridge with force
that came from hate. So much hatred in the world,
and not even all this rain will wash it away. There was no remorse.

Outside your window, that moon has sliced across the night sky
towards the mountain; the sky is still black around its shadow.
Your meadow is rustling with wet creatures scrambling through the wet grass,
and all I can think to tell myself is this pain will pass, this pain will pass.
And indeed there will be time, Eliot said. But will there?
Time to lie inside your hammock dreaming,
to dip naked in that mountain pool we know.
To go boating across to Lime Bay, and not look back.
Time to know that time is not always on your side (you know this).

Would it be worth it to have baked cakes, and set the table for tea,
called the shearers in from the shed, made the bed and made the bed
and made the bed? The rumpled sheets are what I wanted, the sweat
and shame and joy. But there was love in there somewhere. Inside
the cakes, the knitting, the taking up of hems. There was, and I miss it.

I don't hear any mermen singing each to each
though I have spent a large portion of my life on the beach
and would sing back.
Perhaps they have ears only for each other
the way my father had ears only for my mother.
Perhaps I've never listened with the right ears,
or have stopped them up with the wax of fear.

Mermaids seem to have the life, swimming all day,
then sitting on a rock brushing their hair,
making up novel siren songs to lure men into their lair;
they're happy in the two realms.
What happens when you lose someone you love beyond all other care?
Are they there beside you, inside you, or are you holding onto air?
We've all become, in one way or another, bondmaids and slaves;
the wants and woes of worldliness keep us bound beneath the waves.
But some days it seems almost possible to swim up and up
and climb out into the light.

This poem owes an obvious debt to T.S. Eliot

Voice

I'd like to find a case for my voice,
you know the ones,
hard black cover
velvet lining
a sturdy handle
and perhaps a little lock
to chain it to my wrist.
There's the fear, you see,
that I'll leave it on a bus
and when I go to the bus depot
and ask at Lost and Found
they say what sort of voice,
what size, what shape?
Oh, you know, sort of plain.
It's rather cumbersome,
a little shiny, awkward really.
They bring out a trombone
and I shake my head.
Maybe a bit smaller, they say,
or bigger?
They bring out a euphonium.
No, I say, less smooth.
By now there's a queue,
and then the man out the back calls out,
There's one more,
but it's been here so long
we thought no one wanted it.

Winter solstice

The shortest day, one degree,
and all our pagan parts in worship:
nude swimmers at Long Beach right on sunrise,
effigies to burn in the Bacchanalian night.
Out on the water you will still be sleeping,
rocked in the cradle of your boat,
your life afloat on a dream.
I'm drinking your cocoa left at my house
and eating dark chocolate for breakfast.
What is it about a day like this
that sends blood shouting through your veins?
It's as if every nerve is straining
towards the coming light
and all the bones inside you shine.
Aliveness: that's the thing. Love and work.
The Brandenburg concerto number four is on the radio:
If Bach is not in heaven, I'm not going, William F. Buckley said,
and nor am I, but today heaven is here,
that tiny tilt of axis bringing home our miracle.
Now Mischa Meike is singing on his cello
and I give thanks for tiny waves of sound
and the thousand filaments inside an ear.
And now, the symphony Mahler wrote
as a love letter to his future wife:
love, like light, everywhere you look.
Tonight, we will be drinking wine,
listening to drums and cello.
The black moon will sit in its silver cradle
and Venus will shine
while the city throws a bright sabre through the night.

We are burning fears and woes,
welcoming the light.
Oh, the light: today it gilds all things,
the mountain's snow-spangled top,
white hulls of yachts anchored in the estuary,
the red tin roofs of houses;
and the sky is the sort of blue that makes you cry.
I can't help happiness any more than sadness,
only welcome it like the lengthening days,
and say everything I feel to you, listening.
I will hold your hand towards the fire
and you will kiss me right there in the world
as if we belong.
And now, a choir sings a line by e e cummings:
I thank you god for most this amazing day.

Footpaths of desire

You are still on my mind

You are still on my mind.
The silence is eloquent.
The silence is elephants.
There is no room for elephants in the room.
Did I tell you about the seismologist
from the university up the road,
who packed his delicate instruments
and went to Africa to listen to elephants?
Once he'd felt those lumbering love songs
there was no going back to the rattling earth.
He wanted to learn to listen with his toes.
He wanted to learn the things an elephant knows.
It doesn't mean there isn't love in the air,
just because we can't hear it.
He stands still a lot now, feet planted firmly,
and people might think he's lost.
The thing is, he's found,
in the ground beneath him,
the air all about him.

Mudskipper

I've become a mudskipper,
breathing through my skin.
I flex my tail to skip through the day,
pectoral fins to drag myself through the night.
I'm adapting to changed circumstance,
the muddiness of life.
Mudskippers engage in mouth-to-mouth combat,
kissing to fight.
This is a good strategy.
English has more than a million words,
yet I can't find the right ones to say to you.

Night sky

It's a sky for making love beneath.
You know the kind: midnight blue,
light at the horizon,

and the warm breath of air
like a softened solar wind.
Skin is made for this:

an eiderdown of the multiverse,
starshine illuminating every curve and line.
Tonight, the moon is half an ancient silver coin,

something to be touched or worn,
an earring to pierce that gleaming earlobe,
or pendant to hang between those breasts.

Tonight, it can make you happy simply to look up.
Okay, it's all illusion: space is cold.
If you fall into it, the outcome is grave.

You will not freeze;
a vacuum cannot transfer body heat.
But all the air in your lungs

will rush out to fill the void.
At most, you have fifteen seconds.
The more air, the faster it rushes,

obliterating your larynx:
in such a crisis, do not take a deep breath.
What would you say anyway? Goodbye?

The last thing you'll remember
before you fall unconscious
is saliva boiling on your tongue.

Yet here we are, safe, standing still
while hurtling through space
at 107 thousand kilometres an hour,

scraps of being, able to know this,
able to kiss beneath stars
as if it matters.

Nodding greenhood orchid

(Pterostylis nutans)

Today's first surprise:
slender stems emerge from the track,
graceful curves, translucent back,
the nodding greenhood orchid doing just that,
nodding in the slight warm breeze.
Delicate bloom, gracile beauty,
with fluting hood and slender throat,
tempting flies inside with fake red carrion.
I sit and watch for the afternoon
then stretch out on my usual boulder,
once come asunder, thundering down
from the summit like that recent one
on the Zigzag Track.
This one is my friend now, my lover,
bare skin against its hot stone flank.
Aeons rush into me, the fire and cool, the crush,
dissolving fear of time's push.
That rock heart gently mends my own.
I do that thing the Japanese have a name for:
gazing through fractal branches
at fragments of light.
Two birds begin calling to each other –
wren and raven –
and I wonder if raven is as different from wren
as Japanese is from English, or more.
But this is clearly conversation, perhaps duet.
I kiss the rock before I leave
as humans have through millennia:
there were always sacred stones.

The mountain is putting my parts together,
giving me back to myself.

Footpaths of desire

I spend my time making labyrinth designs:
it's not that I plan on getting lost,
instead, on getting found.
The sound of footsteps
echoes in my head at all hours.
That's how I learn of wayfinding:
how to take everything into account –
the way light falls, land undulates,
wind rustling heads of crops –
before you take your next step.
Remember what Theodore Roethke said:
I learn by going where I have to go.
We follow footpaths of desire,
feeling our way into the world,
into its complex dimensions.
We don't leave a trail of breadcrumbs,
or torn-up notebooks, or rice:
we have no plans to return.
What is the point of doing things twice?
And there's the rub:
we want the right path, but there's none.
Only a way forward. One step, another.
The light there, see? On the she-oak tree?
The wind on the ocean's deep swell.
The super moon rising over eastern hills.
Sap is rising; you are rising too,
and must simply trust that where you go
is where you need to go.
Sometimes, that is too much to ask.
But you walk into the unknown
because that's all there is.

Sea creatures

Inveigle yourself into the lives of marine biologists
and accept all sea creatures lovingly into your life.
Adopt the radial symmetry of the sea star,
each of its five tentacles a complete life support system:
this way you will never find yourself wanting or falling short.
Embrace a new perspective as you somersault along the seabed
where life constantly tips you over,
righting yourself each time without effort or grudge.
Your mouth is at the centre of your body; acknowledge this.
Swim out of your depth; swim as far as you dare and then some.
Or try the octopus for size; it has three whole hearts
and seems better equipped for holding on. Use its extreme
intelligence to get you out of tricky situations, tight squeezes;
it knows whether a cave will suit without going inside:
you don't have to learn *everything* through experience.

The Before Midnight Scholar

First, he attaches her toes,
smooth brown cowries in two rows
of descending size.
I could *eat* them! he says.
I *will* eat them! And he does:
first the big toe, so crucial
to her balance, then the smaller ones,
hammertoes saved from surgery,
and last, the tiniest,
smooth little piglet
travelling home safe.

He unearths her feet from layers of wear,
like knobbly new potatoes in soft earth.
He dusts them off, softens their hard yards with kisses.
He heals the childhood chisel scar
with a single touch of his tongue.

He constructs her ankles,
fitting all the little bones together
like a model train-set or a wind-up toy.
He finds the lost key and sets them running.

Her shins appear like magic,
drawn like squid beaks from the body tube,
a fishy miracle of elasticity and strength.
They swim away, changing colour
to suit their mood.

He returns her knees,
kneecaps like Tibetan singing bowls
upended in the palms of his big hands, ringing.

Between her thighs he conjures an inland sea,
late rains rushing down empty river courses,
in the river beds seeds and eggs, life-in-waiting;
vivid flowers and wildlife teem from sleep,
a bounty brought by the touch of rain.
He is the rain.
Birds will arrive in their thousands,
alerted by some knowledge of what is;
they will nest and mate in a rush,
staking claim on a future.
But nothing could be further from the now of instinct,
futures folded away with their wings.

He explores the moonscape of her belly:
one small step for the man,
a giant step for the woman.
He discovers her navel out of place,
abandoned by a careless surgeon;
he sets about adjusting it:
three centimetres to the left;
there, he centres her.
He plants kisses all the way along her scars,
a garden of kisses
that grow long tendrils inside her,
winding up toward her nipples
and creeping out along the lattice
of her nervous system.

Her breasts had been abandoned,
like an old house,
windows smashed and boarded up,
graffiti on the walls.
They might have been condemned
but he determines to resurrect them.
He does it with an architect's attention to detail
and a secret set of tools.
Now they are as good as new.

He withholds nothing, gives back everything,
her shoulders, her arms.
She is able to hold again,
instead of holding on.

Her hands he articulates finger by finger,
giving each one a name and special tasks.
He plays them like a xylophone,
and her tunes flow out into the night air.

My heart was in my mouth, he says.
But now it is up against hers,
beating, strong like a taiko drum,
solemn, then heady,
ceremonial.

Her eyes have been only mirrors,
reflecting badly on everything.
Now he settles them in, like pets,
like sleepy puppies on a rug.

He replaces her ears with small abalone shells,
silvered and glinting in the full moon's shine;
He makes promises:
she will hear the sea wherever she goes;
she will remember the sound of his breath.

Their mouths become happy snails, playing,
gastropods revelling in the wet.

Her hair is, thread by thread, renewed,
a messy skein woven into shining cloth
which warms them both.

This is *thrilling*! he tells her,
giving back not only her body
but words to go with it.

By moonlight, with her new mouth,
she reads Li Yu aloud to him.
The full moon lays a silver path
across the black river.
Later, they say, they will take a walk along it,
now she has her body back.

N.B. The title of this poem comes from the name of a three-hundred-year-old
Chinese book of erotic literature by Li Yu, but the poem owes a debt of memory to
Ted Hughes' poem, *Bride and Groom Lie Hidden for Three Days*.

The mother

For Jane

They call her the mother,
this carefully tended jar of nothing
but flour and water, space and time.
All the yeast we did not know
was in the air and wheat and us
settles into the bowl
and changes the relationship,
like a love affair.
Fermentation, that happy accident of nature,
like sex, is making everything happen.
They put her in the fridge,
guard her secret,
keep others away.
No one is to know what made her
who she is.
All sorts of things get added
as ever more is required of her –
she should be more nutritious, grainier, longer-lasting,
tastier, toastier, full of goodness.
Hail Mary mother of us all,
give us this daily bread.
Oh yes religion is mixed in there too.
Think of the wafer at communion
giving us a taste for heavenly bread,
teaching us to expect god in odd places.
They inspect her daily for signs of decay,
take from her whenever they want,
put just a little back.
They sniff for that yeasty smell,

hope everything will turn out.
Really, they expect her to go on forever.
Some take their mother on holidays with them,
keep feeding her, loath to leave her home alone
in case she dies or turns bad.
Others farm her out to friends,
hope they are conscientious carers.
Extremely old mothers are kept under lock and key,
family heirlooms, only whispered about.
But mostly the mothers do what's required
and when their time is up,
they're out on their own.

The Stingray

for Gina

You've forgotten about poetry.
You tell your friend about the stingray
seen twice on consecutive days
at your usual beach.
You know it's the same one –
it says, Hi! with a Mexican wave from its wings –
and she tells you she swam above it
and wrote a poem.
She learned parts and names,
habits too. How a female can store sperm
for years until the time's judged right for small fry.
In Malaysia, fried is how they eat these fish
(they're really sharks),
with a special sambal sauce.
You've forgotten all this,
how a poem makes you notice more,
makes you seek what nags at your mind
and brings you more joy than almost anything
other than seeing stingray wings flow
to row itself across the sandy bottom of your beach.
Shuffle your feet, the website says. Let them know you're there.
Never startle one – it will flick its barbed tail.
Steve Irwin's ray hit him in the intercostals,
a whiplash to the heart he must have known was coming.
You've forgotten about poetry
but now you feel it coming towards you across a sandy sea floor,
only eyes and tail visible.
But the body is there somewhere, too, and you are shuffling your feet.

Sweet dreams

όνειρα γλυκά
for Ioanna
"The truth is, we know so little about life, we don't really know what the
good news is and what the bad news is." Kurt Vonnegut

The good news is that I have met you;
a weekend spent gleaning slices of your life:
griefs, heartbreaks, joys.
And, throughout, your quiet, enduring heart.
To me you are a Greek heroine
whose persistence through famine and war
overcame every obstacle.
We both know there's a flipside to hardship:
sometimes the worst things in our lives
are the best things in our lives.
Remember *The book of the Samurai?*
There is something to be learned from the rainstorm.

Your friends drop by out of the blue
and, together, you tell the wedding story,
how the bride danced along the street
into everyone's lives.
They say, *She brought him out of himself*
when we thought he was stuck in there.
Γλυκιά ιστορια, I say, and we smile at each other,
at the secret language we've begun.
And who, or what, would bring me out of myself?
Perhaps this? A new language.

You are learning another language, too —
the hidden language of seeds.

Each Monday, your microscope reveals
native seeds' intricate shape, colour, size.
The seeds lie dormant in your hand,
on the microscope film, in their envelope.
You learn the common, then the complex name,
the one which spells out family and connection.
You decipher that name through your own language,
embedded in blood and skin,
woven into your body at the breast.
You learn what every tiny seed's spiralling DNA
will bring to life,
and each one waits for you to send it
on its way to becoming itself.

You are like these seeds:
so much knowledge, love, learning, wisdom
enfolded into one small space –
you haven't even noticed.
You, too, have many names,
like a princess in a fairy-tale.
You choose which version of yourself
you want to live with.
But a new friend has to guess
which name belongs to the real you.
How to become oneself?
That's what we speak about.
How to grow into that mature plant, that tree.
How to flower. How to send our own seeds
into the world.
We return to our topic again and again,
persistent seekers unravelling a difficult rune.
Meanwhile, I say the things that I can say:
Εισαι πολύ γλυκιά *(you are very sweet)*;
όνειρα γλυκά.

Mouna

For Shanti and Gina

The women are walking, silent and single file,
on earth leavened with she-oak needles,
on honeycomb stone, then sand.
Their feet are kissing the world;
the world is kissing back.
A breeze shivers in gum leaves
and she-oak trees, licks waves;

sea tickles the shore.
Gulls play with the lifting air,
hovering with wings spread, then soaring.
They call to each other about the morning.
The sky is lit as if by fire
and the women feel awe for this spinning earth
which feels so still, so calm.

The air is crunchy with cold and salt.
It is dawn; houses are quiet, unlit.
The women attend:
one sees a corner of purple urchin shells,
their finely patterned porcelain;
one is noticing sea snail calligraphy
and blown sea foam caught in rock pools.

One is drawn by the round coral reef
forming on an island of stone.
And another falls in love with sandstone,
its sculpted caves and colours;

on one tawny flank are initials, hearts, names of lovers,
everyone wanting to leave a trace.
The women leave only footprints in wet gold sand

which the tide will soon hide away in itself.
The two altos are listening, singing silently,
There is so much magnificence near the ocean,
waves are comin' in, waves are comin' in.
They are singing in harmony, mind to mind
mind to earth, and smile at each other,
They are like-minded,

in love now with their bodies in this landscape.
They are mothers, lovers, daughters, grandmothers:
they are nature themselves, they remember.
The sky plays with pinks and oranges,
glowing above them like a living entity,
not a fixture of physics and particles of light.
An aeroplane comes banking in;

its passengers have seen the sun
ahead of time, like visionaries, time travellers.
From those glinting windows, the women look tribal,
exploring that shore,
gathering limpets, oysters, mussels.
In truth, they are worshipping the world,
their Mother Earth.

And now they stand to stare at the brightening sky.
They stand like pagans on a flat world
and feel in their bodies
the imminent rise of the sun god.

And there it is, the life-giving sun,
gold breaching the horizon,
rising into their lives,

making the day.
Suddenly, the women throw long shadows,
living gnomons on the sundial of earth.
They might be megaliths at Avebury,
or Stonehenge. They could stand here all day
and time itself would swing around them.
Namaste, their teacher says. *I bow to the light within you.*

And they bow to the light within her.
There is so much light.
Light on the leaves, among the waves,
on the women's faces,
glancing off windows of houses on the point.
It is always about light.
Behind them, a pardalote in a she-oak tree

breaks into morning song.
The day's work has begun.
Snakes shed skins from the mouth out;
these women shed from every cell,
leaving behind an old self,
bearing witness to a new beginning.
Where have they been all their lives?

Notes

Lady Gwendoline: Lady Gwendoline was bought by Tasmanian businessman and former Kingborough Council mayor Don Hazell for his wife, Gwendoline, on their 60th wedding anniversary.

Larnax with octopus: A larnax is a clay burial chest from Minoan culture. MONA – The Museum of Old and New Art – has one.

The girl with her hair towards heaven: This work was part of the MONA exhibition *Theatre of the World*.

The peach orchard of immortality: The geode which inspired this poem was part of the MONA *Monanisms* exhibition.

Rowing down the Nile: This poem is a tribute to Rosemary Mahoney, author of *Down the Nile*, an account of her 1998 120-mile solo journey down the Nile in a seven-foot rowboat.

Sweet dreams: *Hagakure*: *The Book of the Samurai* by Yamamoto Tsunetomo

Mouna: or Mauna, is Hindi for silence, and is often a practice of keeping silent from evening till after breakfast. The song lyrics are by Sw Prem Anubhava from the Osho Song Book. And, in this case, the song has been taught by the fabulous Jane Christie-Johnston of Hobart community choir *Sing For Your Life*.

Acknowledgements

Poems in this collection have previously appeared in *Island, Hecate, Famous Reporter*, the Newcastle Poetry Prize Anthology *Now you shall know*, and a Queensland Poetry Festival Anthology.

This project was assisted by Arts Tasmania and also by the Australia Council.

www.ingramcontent.com/pod-product-compliance
Lightning Source LLC
Chambersburg PA
CBHW030841090426
42737CB00009B/1065